Creepy Crawlies

Worms

Siân Smith

Raintree

www.raintreepublishers.co.uk
Visit our website to find out more information about Raintree books.

To order:
☎ Phone 0845 6044371
▤ Fax +44 (0) 1865 312263
▨ Email myorders@raintreepublishers.co.uk

Customers from outside the UK please telephone +44 1865 312262

Raintree is an imprint of Capstone Global Library Limited, a company incorporated in England and Wales having its registered office at 7 Pilgrim Street, London, EC4V 6LB – Registered company number: 6695582

Text © Capstone Global Library Limited 2013
First published in hardback in 2013
Paperback edition first published in 2014
The moral rights of the proprietor have been asserted.

Edited by Dan Nunn, Rebecca Rissman, and Sian Smith
Designed by Joanna Hinton-Malivoire
Picture research by Ruth Blair
Originated by Capstone Global Library Ltd
Production by Victoria Fitzgerald
Printed and bound in China

ISBN 978 1 406 24142 6 (hardback)
16 15 14 13 12
10 9 8 7 6 5 4 3 2 1

ISBN 978 1 406 24156 3 (paperback)
17 16 15 14 13
10 9 8 7 6 5 4 3 2 1

British Library Cataloguing in Publication Data
Smith, Sian.
  Worms. – (Creepy crawlies)
  1. Earthworms–Pictorial works–Juvenile literature.
  I. Title II. Series
  592.6'4-dc22

Acknowledgements
We would like to thank the following for permission to reproduce photographs: Corbis p.21 (© Robert Pickett); Dreamstime.com pp.6 (© Bernd Lang), 19 (© Raluca Tudor), 22 (© Aetmeister), 23 (© Dreamam); © Dwight Kuhn p.11; istockphoto p.6 (© Vinicius Ramalho Tupinamba); Science Photo Library p.17 (Steve Gschmeissner); Shutterstock pp.5 (© mashe), 7 (© Dusty Cline), 7 (© Milos Luzanin), 8 (© Lipik), 9 (© photolinc), 13 (© Melinda Fawver), 15 (© Zeljko Radojko), 22 (© irin-k), 22 (© Vital Che), 22 (© Henrik Larsson), 23 (© Cameramannz), 23 (© photolinc), 23 (© Alex Staroseltsev).

Front cover photograph reproduced with permission of Dreamstime.com (© Vinicius Tupinamba).

The publisher would like to thank Michael Bright for his help in the preparation of this book.

Every effort has been made to contact copyright holders of any material reproduced in this book. Any omissions will be rectified in subsequent printings if notice is given to the publisher.

Contents

Hiding underground

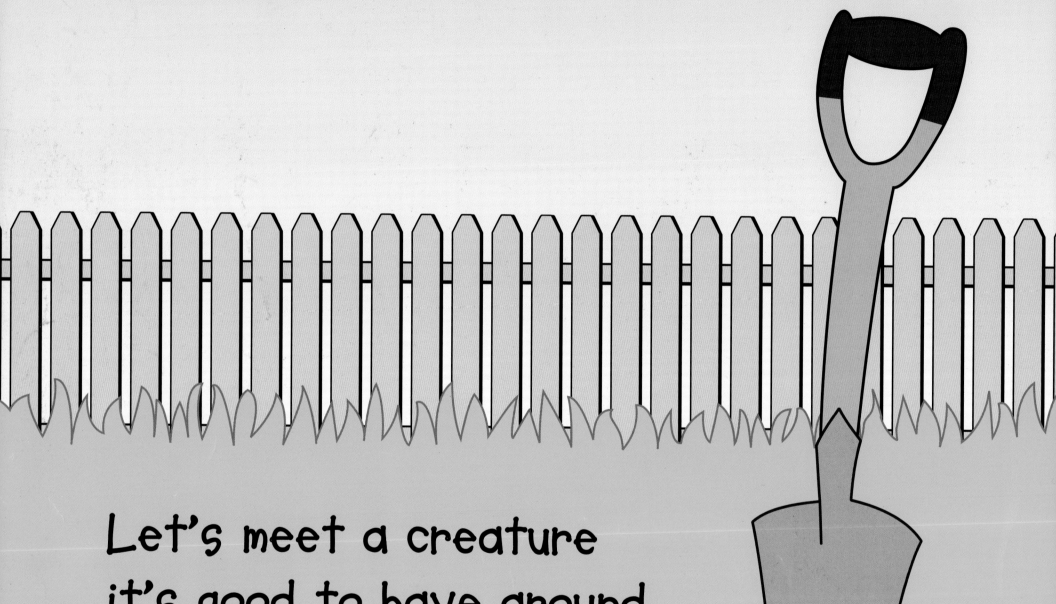

Let's meet a creature
it's good to have around.

The best way to find one
is to dig in the ground.

It's long, thin, and slimy.
What is it, do you think?

That's right! It's a worm,
and most of them are pink.

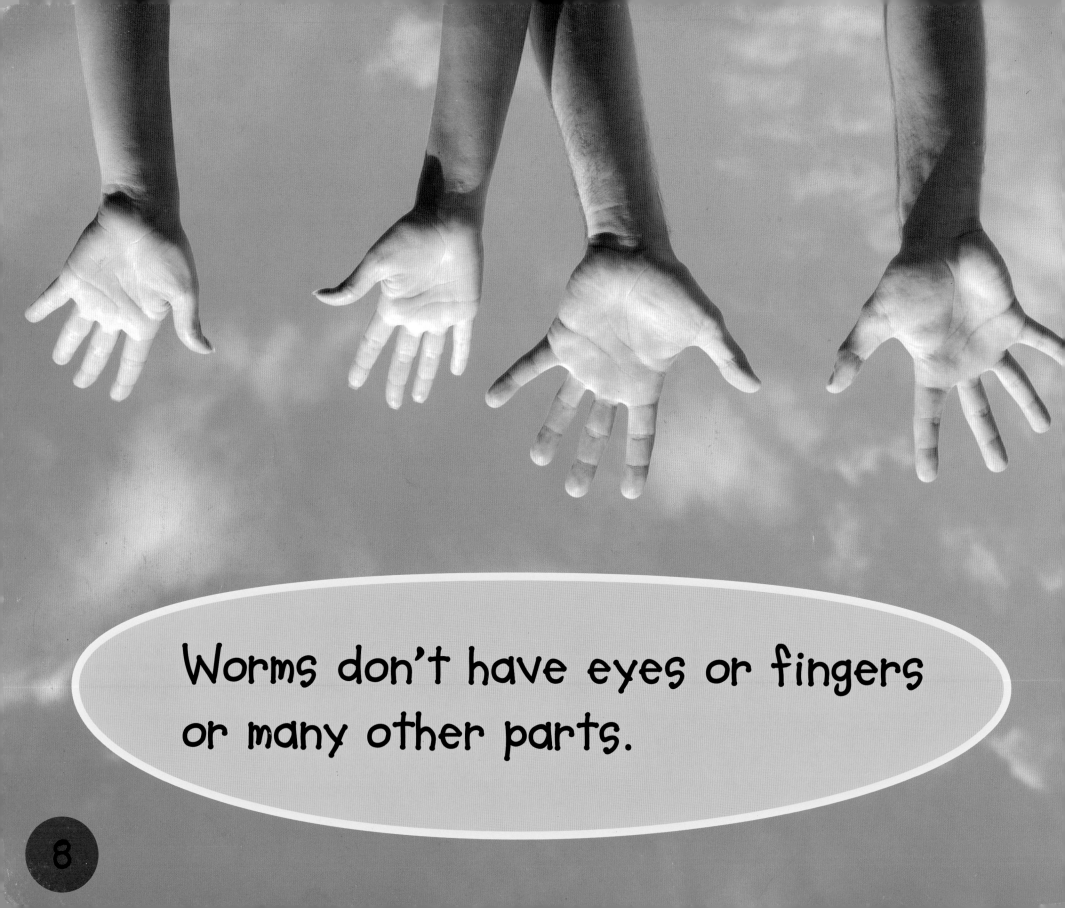

Worms don't have eyes or fingers or many other parts.

But inside a worm's body
it has **five** beating hearts.

A worm does have a mouth, but it's difficult to see.

This worm's opened its mouth to eat a leaf from a tree.

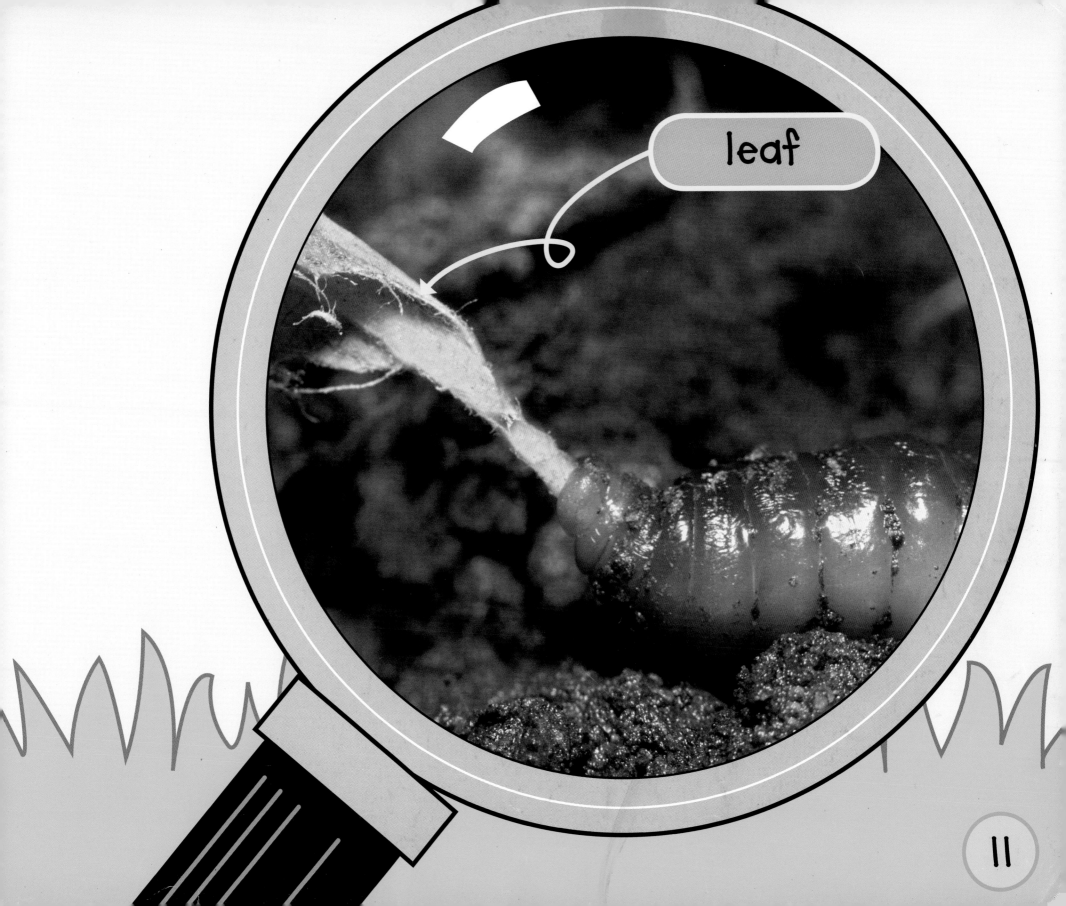

leaf

Worm breath

Worms don't breathe through a mouth or even through a nose.

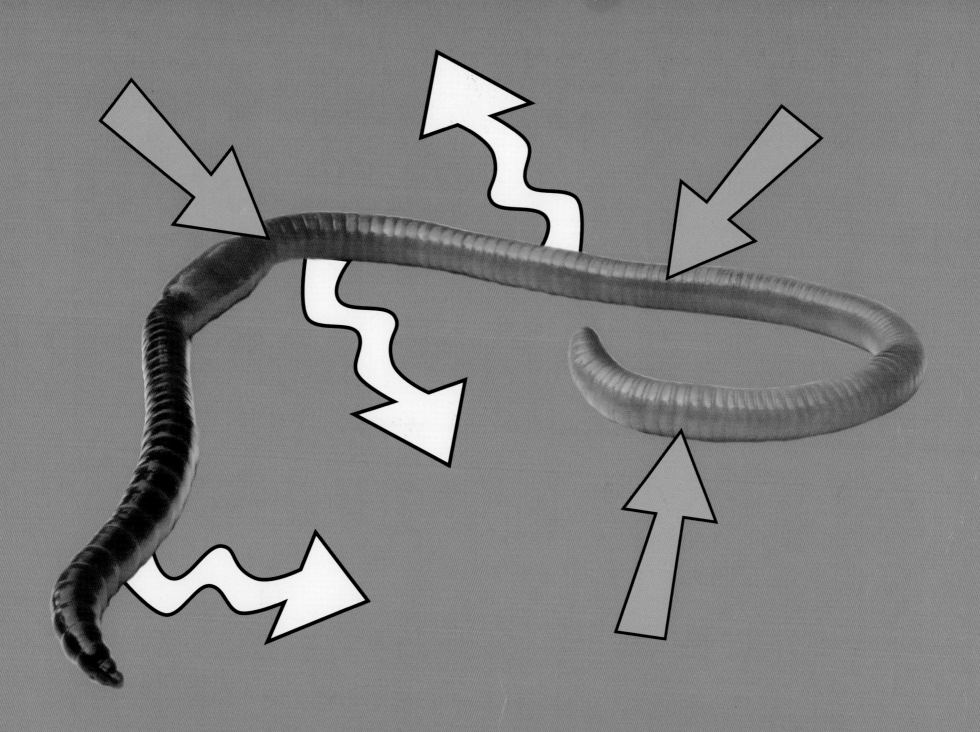

Worms breathe through their skin.
That's where the air goes.

To keep on breathing,
worms need to stay wet.

So a worm is a good choice if you want a slimy pet!

15

Hairy movers

Look at a worm's body closely,
and small hairs can be found.

These help the worm to move,
as it wriggles around.

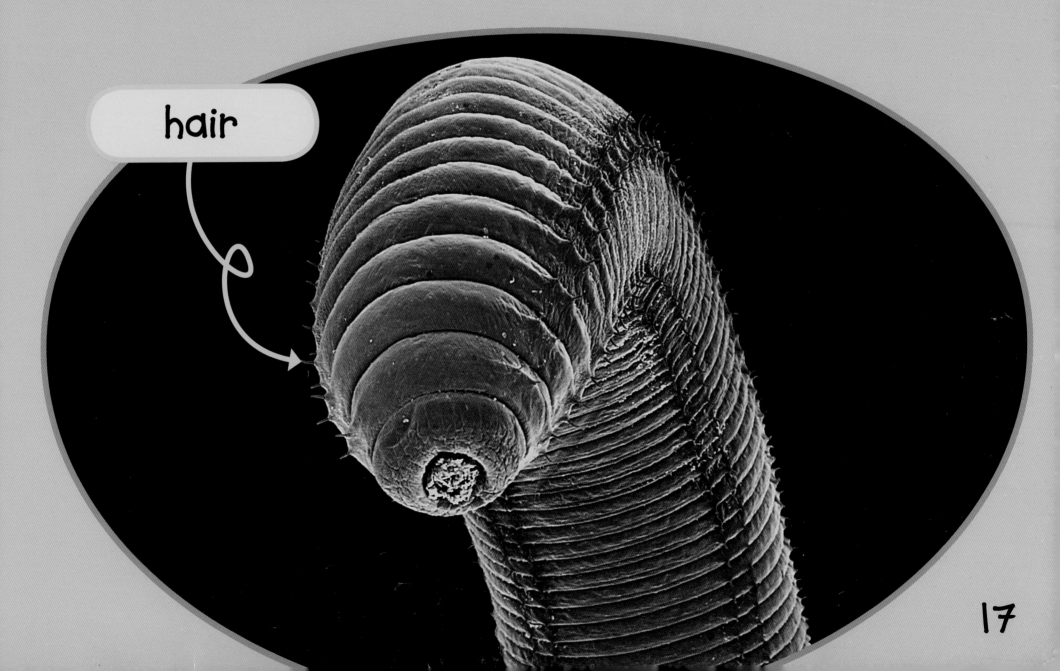

Baby worms

Any two worms can make babies,
and that's really quite nice.

Babies hatch out of cocoons,
which look like small grains of rice.

19

Squishy brown piles

If you see a brown pile
do you know what you've found?

It comes out of a worm's bottom, but it's good for the ground!

Spot the worm!

Somewhere on this page,
a small worm has hid.

Are you able to find it?
Well done if you did!

Did you know?

A worm's slime is very good for the soil and helps plants to grow.

Index